MANITOUWADGE PUBLIC LIBRARY

FRIENDLY BEES,
FEROCIOUS BEES

FRIENDLY BEES, FEROCIOUS BEES

BY MONA KERBY

FRANKLIN WATTS | 1987 | A FIRST BOOK
NEW YORK | LONDON | TORONTO | SYDNEY

FRONTIS: BEE
DRINKING NECTAR FROM
A CLOVER FLOWERHEAD

Artwork by Anne Canevari Green

Photographs courtesy of
© Jerome Wexler/Photo Researchers: pp. 2, 62;
U.S. Department of Agriculture photo by B. Carnahan: p. 8;
The Metropolitan Museum of Art (30.4.88): p. 10;
U.S. Department of Agriculture photo by William P. Nye: p. 18;
U.S. Department of Agriculture photo: pp. 24, 25
(bottom), 59, 61, 73; © Stephen Dalton/Photo Researchers:
pp. 25 (top), 26, 31, 36, 38, 39, 42, 67, 74;
© Colin G. Butler, F.R.P.S./Photo Researchers: p. 45;
New York Public Library Picture Collection: pp. 47, 68;
UPI/Bettmann Newsphotos: p. 71.

Library of Congress Cataloging-in-Publication Data

Kerby, Mona.
Friendly bees, ferocious bees.

(A First book)
Bibliography: p.
Includes index.
Summary: Describes the physical characteristics, habits, and
natural environment of honeybees and Africanized bees.
Also discusses beekeeping and includes recipes using honey.
1. Honeybee—Juvenile literature. 2. Brazilian
honeybee—Juvenile literature. 3. Bee culture—
Juvenile literature. 4. Cookery (Honey)—Juvenile
literature. [1. Honeybee. 2. Brazilian honeybee.
3. Bee culture. 4. Cookery—Honey] I. Title.
QL568.A6K425   1987   595.79′9   86-22479
ISBN 0-531-10303-X

CONTENTS

Chapter 1
Apis Mellifera
9

Chapter 2
Parts of the Honeybee
12

Chapter 3
The Queen, the Drones, and the Young
23

Chapter 4
Life of the Hive
34

Chapter 5
Communication
49

Chapter 6
Beekeeping
54

Chapter 7
Diseases and Enemies
63

Chapter 8
Killer Bees
70

Chapter 9
Bee Hunts
78

Chapter 10
Cooking with Honey
83

Glossary
90

For Further Reading
93

Index
94

Acknowledgments

I am grateful to Dr. Orley Taylor
of the University of Kansas, who
directs the United States Department
of Agriculture's investigation of
the killer bees, for his generous loan
of research reports and his very
helpful review of Chapter 7.

Apis mellifera,
which means "honey-bearer"

APIS MELLIFERA

We are supposedly the smartest species on Earth. Yet, we know relatively little about most other species.

Take, for instance, honeybees. Some people live an entire lifetime and know just two things about them—that they sting and that they make honey.

The scientific name for honeybees is *Apis mellifera*, which means "bee honey-bearer." But did you know that bees die when they sting you? Did you know that bees have jobs? Did you know that bees air-condition their homes and have done so for millions of years? Did you know that bees communicate with each other? Did you know that not only are honeybees the only insects that produce a food humans eat, but also that they produce one of the purest foods in the world?

For at least 17,000 years, humans have risked getting stung for the pleasure of eating honey. In 15,000 B.C., an unknown artist drew a picture on a cave in Valencia, Spain. The picture showed two men climbing up to a beehive. One held a basket. Bees buzzed around him as he robbed the hive. In 3,000 B.C., Egyptian tombs were inscribed with pictures of honeybees. Honey was found in some of those tombs.

*Egyptian tomb painting, entitled "Honey Gathering,"
from the reign of Rehkmire, eighteenth dynasty*

It was still good. The Bible referred to a "land of milk and honey." Athletes in the early Greek Olympics ate honey for energy. And Aristotle, the famous Greek philosopher, wrote that honey is "a dew distilled from the stars and rainbow." Early people knew that honey was delicious and healthy.

Throughout the centuries, these insects have fascinated people. Many scientists have studied them. Much of what was once believed to be true was found false. Democritus, a Greek philosopher before Aristotle's time, wrote that if you wanted some bees, you should kill an ox and lock it up for thirty-two days. Bees would come from the ox, he declared. As late as 1842, some people still believed that to be true.

We know more about honeybees today. In this book, you will learn what scientists know about honeybees. You will learn how a bee makes honey. You will learn how the queen, the workers, and the drone bees live together. You will learn about the dances of bees, how to get started in beekeeping, how killer bees endanger U.S. agriculture, and even how to cook with honey. After you have read this book, you will be wiser than the wisest beekeepers of a hundred years ago.

But there are still certain mysteries about honeybees. How does each bee know what job to do? If scientists know the ingredients of beeswax, why can't they reproduce it? How can a tiny honeybee, with a brain less than half the size of a grain of rice, "tell" another bee where there is food? The facts we know provide only small clues to the larger mysteries.

2

PARTS OF
THE HONEYBEE

Have you ever seen a honeybee? If you have, then more than likely you saw a female, a worker honeybee. Most of the bees in a hive are female. There aren't many male bees, or drones, in a hive. In a strong, healthy hive, there will be one queen bee (a female), a couple of hundred drones, and nearly 50,000 worker bees.

These worker bees are amazing. Perhaps the most amazing thing about them is that they can actually turn the nectar of flowers into honey. They are the only insects in the world that produce a food both for themselves and for humans. The delicious sweet honey that you spread on your toast was made for you by insects. Think of that!

To turn nectar into honey, bees first of all must find flowers that have nectar and pollen. Second, they must be able to transport the nectar and pollen. Third, they must be able to locate, and then return to, the hive.

Worker bees' bodies are designed perfectly for such tasks. Take, for example, the bees' eyes. Honeybees have five eyes. Three single eyes sit on top of the head in a triangular pattern and two "compound" eyes sit on each side of the head. There are more than 3,000 lenses in each of those compound eyes. Their eyes recognize the colors blue, yellow, and green and can see ultraviolet light. They can see flowers. They can recognize landmarks. And, they can recognize their home hive.

In this chapter, you will learn the parts of the honeybee. As you read, remember that these intricate parts are found on an insect that is less than 1 inch (2.5 cm) long. Amazing!

EXOSKELETON

Like all insects, the honeybee has an exoskeleton. Whereas our skeletons are on the inside of our bodies, the honeybee skeleton is on the outside. Stronger than bone and lighter in weight, it protects the insides of the bee.

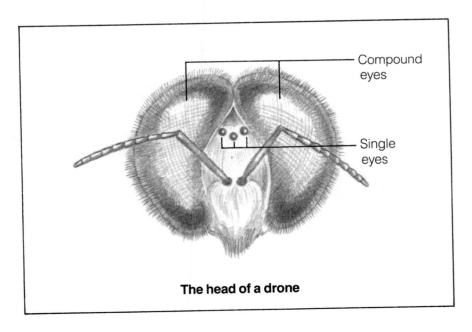

Compound eyes

Single eyes

The head of a drone

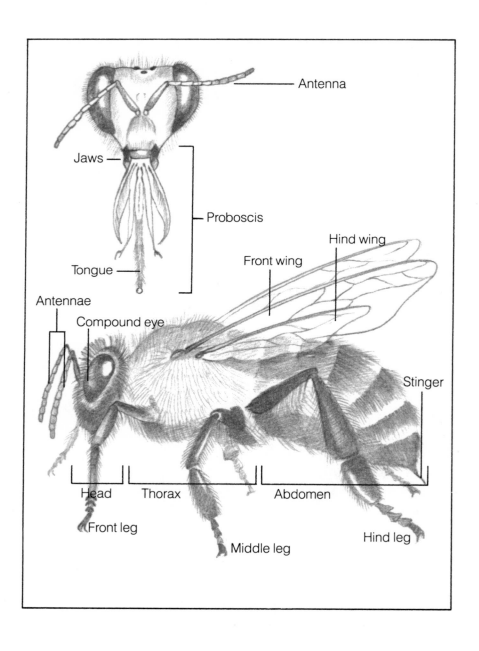

If the exoskeleton were one solid piece, moving would be difficult. However, the bee is divided into three distinct sections: the head, the thorax, and the abdomen. Each part narrows where it joins the next section. As a result, somewhat of a hinge is formed that allows the bee to bend.

A bee has a thick coat of fluffy hair that covers the exoskeleton. This hair catches and holds pollen for the bee as she (and most often it is a "she") flies from flower to flower.

HEAD

In addition to the eyes, two antennae are located on the bee's head. These move freely from their individual sockets. Tiny hairs cover the lower segment of each antenna. Antennae help bees to smell, and they may also help bees to hear, feel, and communicate. Bees are constantly cleaning their antennae.

The parts of the mouth also serve a purpose. The tongue is long, hairy, and spoon-shaped at the end. When the bee sips nectar from flowers, or honey or water, her mouth and tongue form a long tube, or proboscis (pronounced pro BÄS kiss). After she finishes, she draws the proboscis up and folds it underneath her head.

Pollen and wax must be softened and wet. The bee accomplishes this by chewing them in her mouth. Her jaws chew sideways rather than up and down, like ours.

The head of a worker bee contains glands that are capable of producing food. The so-called brood food glands produce "royal jelly," a rich, milky-white secretion. Royal jelly is secreted through a worker bee's mouth and is fed to all young bees for the first three days of their life.

THORAX

Positioned on the heavily muscled thorax are the wings and legs. Wings are of the utmost importance to a bee. Without them, she can't fly to the fields to collect nectar and pollen. If she can't do that, she can't make honey.

You might think, then, that her wings would be beautiful and sleek. This is not the case. The wings are short and stubby. They are also very thin. (Bees, wasps, and ants all belong to the order Hymenoptera, which means "membrane wings.") A bee has four wings; two on each side hook together and function as one.

It is somewhat of a surprise that their wings even work. But they work wonderfully well. Their stubby little wings beat from 160 to 200 times a minute. (According to musicians, this is in the key of C sharp, below middle C.) Furthermore, when a bee flies, its wings move up, down, forward, and backward. They can even partially rotate.

Perhaps the biggest surprise is that a honeybee flies at a speed of 15 to 25 miles (24 to 40 km) an hour. In fact, for its weight and size, a honeybee flies faster and farther than any other winged creature in the world.

A honeybee has six legs. We use our legs to walk, and so does a honeybee. But the bee also has some special features on her legs that help her in her work. For example, a honeybee is able to walk equally well on smooth or rough surfaces. When she wants to cling to rough surfaces, she extends small claws, and when she wants to cling to smooth surfaces, she extends small, sticky pads. On her front legs, she has small brushes that she uses to wipe pollen and dust from her eyes. One particularly interesting feature is her antenna cleaner. A bee uses the small semicircular notches on her front legs to clean pollen off each antenna by sliding the antenna through the notch.

Another interesting feature is located on the hind legs. Here, there are large, flat brushes of stiff hairs called pollen baskets. As you might imagine, bees use these baskets for carrying pollen. If you're lucky, you might see a worker bee returning to the hive with the yellow mounds of pollen packed in her pollen baskets.

To get a load of pollen, a bee allows tiny specks of pollen dust to collect all over her hairy body. She then grabs some of this pollen with her tongue and takes it into her mouth, where she moistens it. The front legs clean pollen from the head, the eyes, the mouth, and the antennae. The middle legs take the pollen from the mouth, brush the pollen off the thorax, and pack everything into the baskets on her hind legs. All of this grabbing, moistening, and packing takes place at the same time the bee is flying to the next flower.

A bee will work a long time to collect pollen. On a good day, it will take about ten minutes to gather a load. But on a slow day it may take two hours, and the bee will visit a hundred flowers before she finishes. These loads are very small in human terms. To gather one teaspoonful of pollen would take an average bee six hundred hours!

ABDOMEN

The third and last section of the bee is the abdomen. It includes the honey stomach, stomach, intestine, wax glands, reproductive organs, and sting. A bee's stomach and intestine aid in digestion. In her reproductive organs, a female bee produces eggs. Worker bees have unfertilized eggs that

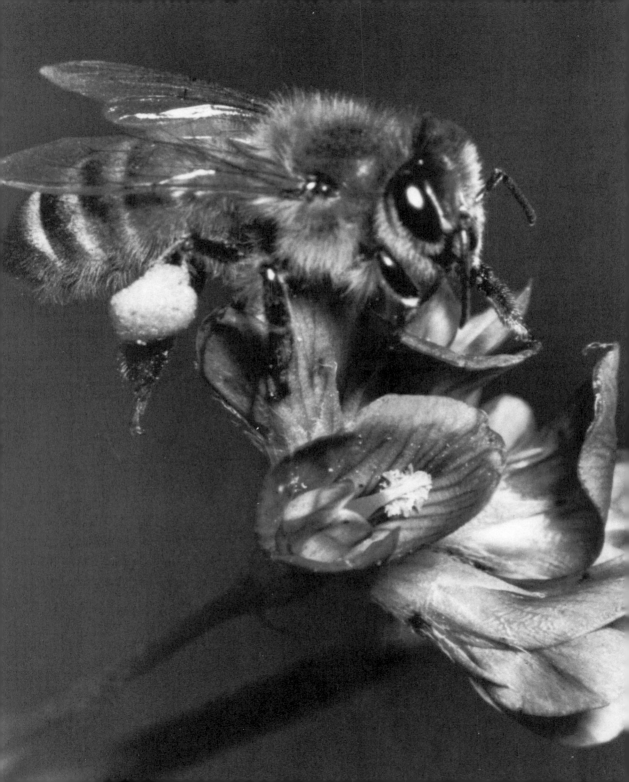

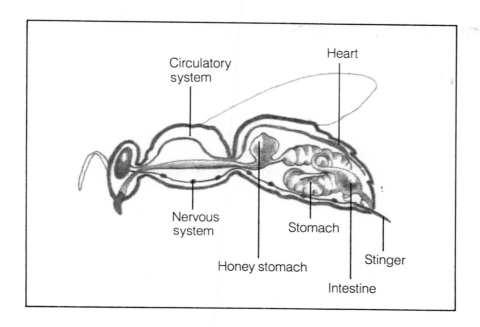

Circulatory system

Heart

Nervous system

Stomach

Honey stomach

Stinger

Intestine

are rarely laid because that is the queen bee's job. But in an emergency, if something happens to the queen, some worker bees will begin laying unfertilized drone eggs until the other workers have produced a new queen.

We mentioned earlier that a bee uses her proboscis to sip nectar from flowers. But do you know where she stores

A bee collects nectar on an alfalfa blossom. Note the load of alfalfa pollen (the white mass) in the pollen basket on the hind leg.

the nectar as she works? She stores it in a specially designed honey stomach. A bee has two stomachs; a valve between the two prevents the nectar from entering her second stomach. She won't use the nectar in her honey stomach unless she needs energy to fly.

The honey stomach is very tiny. Still, to get a full load, a bee may work an hour and a half and visit more than 1,000 flowers. She then deposits her little load of nectar at the hive and returns to the field to collect another drop. Usually, she makes about ten trips per day.

You probably have honey in your kitchen cabinet. And more than likely, you have a 1-pound (.45-kg) jar. Bees flew 50,000 miles (80,000 km) to make that pound of honey. That's a lot of miles.

One of the more fascinating sets of organs in the abdomen are the wax glands. Bees make wax! Somehow their body is able to change honey into a different substance, and that substance is beeswax. Beeswax is used by bees to make cells that store pollen and honey. It is a clean and sanitary material.

To produce wax, the bees first gorge on honey. Then they hook legs with one another and hang quietly. This is called clustering. From this clustering, the temperature in the hive rises. After about twenty-four hours, small flakes of wax appear on the underside of the bees' abdomen. The bees then mold this wax into hexagonal (six-sided) cells. A hexagonal is a very efficient shape for storing honey.

How do bees know that a hexagon—and not a circle, triangle, square, rectangle, octagon, or any other figure—is the ideal shape in which to store honey? We don't know.

But of all the parts of the honeybee, the sting is the most noticeable feature. A bee does not sting because she is mean

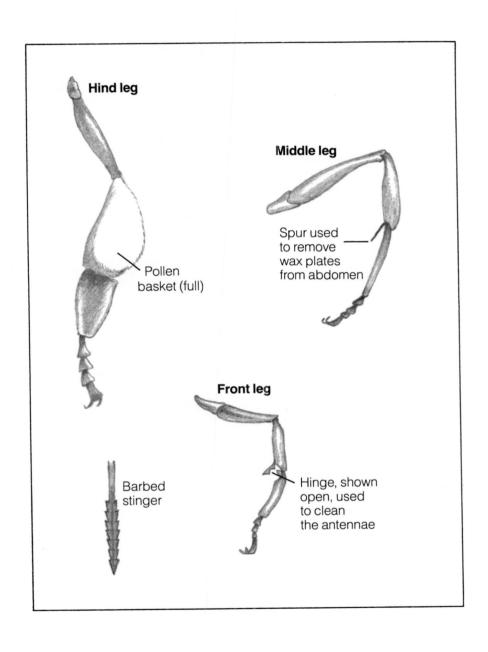

Hind leg

Pollen basket (full)

Middle leg

Spur used to remove wax plates from abdomen

Front leg

Barbed stinger

Hinge, shown open, used to clean the antennae

or because she hates you. She stings as a defense. If she senses that someone or something intends to harm the hive, she will attack with a weapon that causes humans a hundred times larger to run away in terror.

Composed of three segments, the sting is pointed and barbed. Attached to it is a large sac filled with poison. Because the sting is barbed, the bee cannot easily remove it after it has entered your skin. To get away, she is forced to rip the rest of her body from the sting. The sting remains in you, and the bee suffers from a large open wound. Almost always a bee dies after stinging.

The bee's heart is also in the abdomen and controls the bee's circulatory system. Pale, amber-colored blood pumps throughout the bee's body. It distributes food and removes waste materials.

A bee's blood doesn't carry oxygen to different parts of the body as our blood does. A bee breathes differently from the way we do. Ten small openings in the head, the thorax, and the abdomen are connected to tubes that enable a bee to breathe.

A ventral nerve cord runs throughout the length of the bee's body and is attached to the brain, which is located in the head. The brain receives sensory messages from the eyes and the antennae and transmits those messages to the ventral nerve cord. Humans must have brains to function. This is not true for a bee. A bee without a brain can walk, fly, and even sting!

These are the basic parts of the worker honeybee. Although they are similar to the workers in many ways, the queen bee and drones have their own distinct characteristics. The differences that exist among the queen, the workers, and the drones are examined in the next chapter.

3

THE QUEEN, THE DRONES, AND THE YOUNG

The worker bees are so named because they do almost all of the work in the hive. The drones do no work whatsoever, and the only job the queen has is to lay the eggs. However, even though the workers are the most productive bees, they need the queen and the drones in order to survive. In this chapter you will learn about the growth of young bees and the characteristics of the queen and the drones.

THE YOUNG

Baby bees, called brood, go through three stages of growth. The first stage is the egg. After three days, the egg hatches and enters the larval stage.

For the first three days of life, all larvae are fed the rich royal jelly from the workers' brood food glands. After that, although the queen brood continues to be fed the rich royal jelly, worker brood is fed a somewhat undernourishing diet of bee bread, which is a mixture of pollen and honey. Drone brood is fed an even courser mixture of pollen and honey.

Not only is there a difference in diet, but there is also a

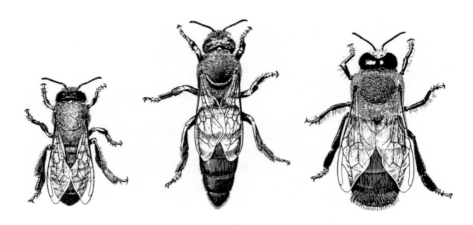

From left to right: worker bee, queen, and drone

difference in the size of the living quarters for the queen, worker, and drone brood. Worker brood is raised in the smallest cells; the cells for drone brood are larger. For the queen cells, workers enlarge a particular worker cell by tearing out the walls of the surrounding worker brood cells and killing the brood occupying them. Queen cells are generally as large as three ordinary worker cells.

When the larvae are fully grown, the workers cap the cells with wax. This is the last stage, called the pupal period. Again, different types of brood are treated differently. Worker brood cells are sealed over smooth and flat. Drone brood cells are capped with a rounded seal. Queen cells have a large thimble-shaped covering.

Top: *eggs of honeybees*
Bottom: *a honeybee*
larva (left) and pupa

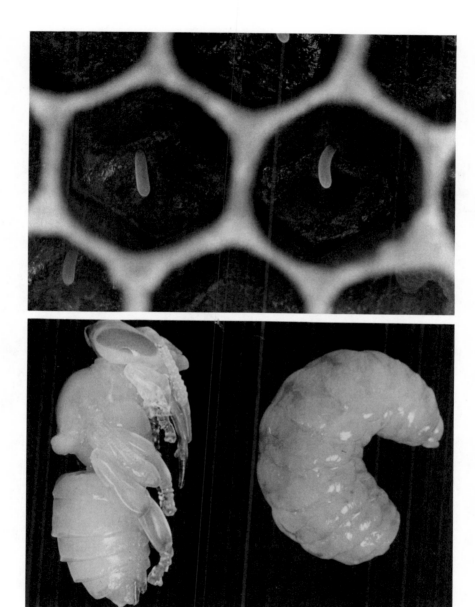

A queen bee emerges from her capped cell

This entire process, from egg to adult bee, takes about three weeks. Young queen bees emerge from capped cells in about sixteen days. Workers emerge in twenty-one days. Drone bees are the last to emerge, at twenty-four days. The chart below shows the developmental stages of the brood.

DEVELOPMENTAL STAGES OF THE BROOD

	Queen	Worker	Drone
	Number of days		
Egg Hatches	3	3	3
Cell Is Capped	8	8	10
Adult Emerges	16	21	24

THE QUEEN

A beehive must have a queen. The queen bee doesn't rule the colony, issuing orders and telling the other bees what to do. In a way, she is more of a prisoner than a monarch. She lives because the workers let her live. They take care of her. She spends almost all of her life laying eggs, hidden in the darkness of the hive.

Nevertheless, the queen bee appears to have a certain royal dignity about her as she moves over the combs. She walks slowly and purposefully. She holds her short wings close to her body. If she is disturbed by anything, such as a beekeeper opening the hive, she will usually retreat and hide until order and darkness return.

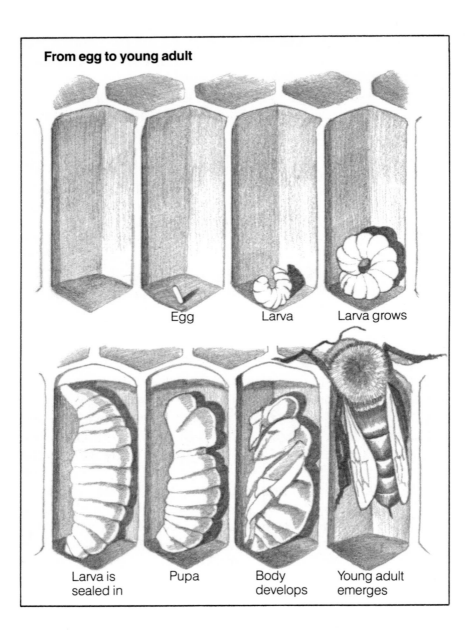

From egg to young adult

Egg

Larva

Larva grows

Larva is sealed in

Pupa

Body develops

Young adult emerges

Always, she is surrounded by her "court." Although membership in this group changes frequently, the court feeds the queen, grooms her, removes her feces, and spreads her smell throughout the hive. The hive and the bees "smell" like the queen.

A queen is different from the other bees in several ways. For one thing, she lives much longer than the workers and the drones. On the average, she lives for one or two years, but she can live five to seven years. She is also physically longer than the other two. Like the workers, the queen bee has a sting, but she rarely uses it on humans. Her large sting has fewer barbs and is more firmly attached to her body. As a result, it can be used repeatedly, and she will not hesitate to use it to kill other queens.

Another way in which the queen is different from the worker bee is that she is unable to gather food. Her tongue is too short to sip nectar, and she has no pollen baskets. Her eyes also don't see as well, having nearly 2,400 fewer fixed lenses than worker bees' eyes. (A queen has approximately 3,900 fixed lenses, while a worker has 6,300.) Furthermore, she has no brood food glands in her head and is unable to feed her children. She can give them life, but she cannot take care of them. The workers must do that.

But the major difference between the queen and the worker bees is that the queen alone mates with a drone. When a new queen bee emerges from her cell, she issues a battlecry, "Z-e-e-p, ze-ep, zeep!" She kills other developing queens by tearing open their cells. If she and another queen emerge at the same time, they will fight and sting each other again and again until one of them dies.

For a few days, none of the other bees pays much attention to the young queen. She wanders around the hive and practices flying outside. Sometime between the fourth and tenth day of her life she is ready to mate.

On a warm spring afternoon, the queen leaves the hive and soars into the air. Hundreds of drones are waiting outside, and when they spot her, they fly after her. The young queen flies up to 15 feet (4.5 m) in the air. At that height, only the drones with the keenest eyesight, sharpest sense of smell, and strongest wings catch her. Those that succeed mate with her in the air.

Perhaps for a few fleeting seconds, the triumphant drone enjoys his victory. Then, whether he delights in his achievement or not, the moment is suddenly over. Part of the drone's body is abruptly ripped away, making a popping sound. With a large gaping hole in his abdomen, the wounded drone falls to the ground and dies.

When the queen returns to the hive, she is now recognized as the true queen. Her court removes from her the remaining parts of the drones' bodies. The queen's lengthy abdomen now holds an average of 5.5 million sperm, more than enough to last her her entire life. That means she has the potential to lay as many as 2,000 eggs daily, or one egg every minute. However, she doesn't produce young at this rate all of the time.

Perhaps what is most astonishing is that the queen bee determines the sex of her young. Humans have never been able to do this with any accuracy, and yet queen bees have done it for thousands of years. In drone cells, the queen bee lays unfertilized eggs, which become male bees. In worker cells, she lays fertilized eggs, which become female bees. In other words, female worker bees have both a father and mother. But the male drone bees have only one parent—their

*Queen honeybee surrounded
by attendant workers*

mother, the queen bee. Now that is certainly different from humans!

THE DRONES

Drones are male bees. They do no work either inside or outside the hive. Inside, they just lie around the combs. Outside, they fly for hours in the warm sunshine. Their sole purpose is to mate with the queen.

Such a leisurely life has its drawbacks. For one thing, it is usually quite brief. During the spring and summer months, several hundred drones are allowed to live. But during the winter months, the worker bees usually kill them all off.

In spite of their short life span of four months, drone bees are physically quite strong. Longer than the worker and shorter than the queen, drone bees are very thick around. With the longest wings, they are powerful fliers. (However, they are clumsy walkers.) Their large eyes cover most of their head and contain 13,000 fixed lenses. For smelling, drones have 37,000 olfactory centers in each antenna. The workers have 500 such centers.

Adult drones have short tongues and no pollen baskets; they are physically incapable of gathering food. Very young drones can feed themselves honey, but they soon lose this ability and must be fed by the workers. Also, even though the loud buzzing noises made by drones sound ferocious, they are unable to defend themselves. Drones cannot sting.

By no means, though, are drones incapable of fulfilling their destiny. For one brief glorious moment, they soar. Nature designed them to fly, seek, and mate with the queen. On the warm spring afternoon of the queen's mating flight, they do just that.

Those that succeed in mating with the queen die instantly. Those that survive the mating flight continue to be fed by the workers for a while. But at summer's end, when there is less nectar and pollen available, the worker bees stop feeding the drones. The half-starved drones are then pulled out of the hive and left to die.

4

LIFE OF THE HIVE

Imagine you are from outer space, and you are hovering over a large Earth city in your spaceship. You see people scurrying to and fro on sidewalks, police officers blowing whistles and moving their hands, children dashing into classrooms, adults entering offices, hospitals, and stores. You wonder if there is any order to this chaos. But you are a patient, curious alien, and you observe the city a little longer. Eventually you see that each person has a place to go and a job to accomplish.

So it is with life in a beehive. Upon first inspection of a hive, you see perhaps 50,000 bees moving about in what appears to be total confusion. But after observing, you discover that there is an intricate order to bee life. Just like people, bees have jobs to accomplish. No one bee controls the hive, yet every bee seems to know what to do. Scientists don't fully understand how bees learn their different jobs; there aren't any bee schools. And scientists don't know why bees work as hard as they do; it appears that the bees are compelled by their biology to sacrifice their lives for the good of the colony. In this chapter, you will learn about the jobs of the worker bees, the seasonal cycles of bee life, and the different kinds of hives.

JOBS INSIDE THE HIVE

For the most part, the bees that work in the hive are the younger ones. At the peak of the spring and summer months, when the nectar flow is at its highest, they will work in the hive for about three weeks, then work outside for another three weeks. Within six weeks, they usually wear themselves out and die. Although there is no rigid division of labor, there is a tendency for bees to do certain jobs according to their ages. The jobs that bees accomplish inside the hive are cell polishing, brood feeding, food storing, comb cleaning, comb building, fanning, and guarding.

Cell Polishing ● Soon after a young worker bee emerges from its cell for the first time, she moves to a cell containing honey and begins eating. When she finishes, she gives herself a thorough cleaning and is ready for her first task— polishing brood cells. This is done by her carefully licking the insides of the cells. The queen will not lay eggs in the brood cells unless they have been cleaned in this manner. Young bees spend approximately three days polishing cells.

Brood Feeding ● Worker bees spend the next ten days of life "nursing," or feeding, the brood. As you already know, worker bees are able to produce food in their heads, and they feed this royal jelly to the young brood. When the larvae are three days old, the nurse bees feed bee bread to worker brood and a courser mixture of pollen and honey to drone brood.

*Bee pupae at different
stages of development*

Nurse bees spend an extraordinary amount of time in caring for the brood. From the time an egg is laid until eight days later, when the cell is capped, nurse bees visit each cell 1,300 times daily, or more than 10,000 visits in all. On the average, 2,785 bees spend ten hours, sixteen minutes, and eight seconds caring for the cell and the larva. Under this care, an egg weighing $\frac{1}{10}$ of a milligram on the first day will weigh 150 milligrams within five days. If a 6-pound (2.7-kg) human baby were cared for in a similar manner, the infant would weigh 4 tons!

Food Storing ● Another job the young bees have is to store the pollen and nectar that has been collected by the field bees, the bees that work outside the hive. After these field bees drop their loads of pollen into the cells, a house bee examines the pollen, then packs it down with her head and mouth. She moistens the pollen with her tongue and combines it with the pollen already in the cell. This mixture is called bee bread.

A different method is used to store nectar. A field bee returning to the hive with nectar opens her mouth to a house bee. The house bee stretches her proboscis and sips the nectar from the other bee.

Both bees constantly touch each other's antennae. To ripen the nectar into honey, the house bee works it in her honey stomach for about twenty minutes, then deposits the drop in a cell. Water must evaporate from the nectar before it becomes honey. In two to five days, when the process is complete, the drops are collected, stored in a cell with other drops, and sealed with a thin layer of wax. In this way, nectar is changed into honey.

Worker honeybees exchanging food

Honey storage cells, capped and uncapped

Comb Cleaning ● By the time a worker bee is approximately fifteen days old, her body quits making royal jelly and she is ready to fly. Outside, she practices flying and locating the hive. Once she learns how to recognize the hive, she starts cleaning the combs. Bees are extremely clean. The cleaning bees collect dead bees, dead brood, the feces of drones and the queen, mold, and any other debris and deposit it several hundred yards from the hive.

Comb Building ● Hundreds of bees help in comb building. First, there are those bees that produce the wax. After the wax forms, in twenty-four hours, it takes only four minutes for the bees to remove the small flakes from the abdomen, chew and soften it, and then stick the small ball to a cell. Some bees mold the wax into a cell. Moments later, other bees gnaw on it. It seems almost as if they work against each other. Bees may work for a mere thirty seconds before stopping to let other bees take over.

Bees construct honeycomb that is nearly perfect in design, a feat that amazes human engineers. The shape, size, and weight of each cell are important factors in this successful structure. The cells are hexagonal (six-sided), for this is the most efficient shape for storing honey. If you think about it, you will realize that a series of circles, triangles, or squares waste space and material. Moreover, all the cells slant downward so that the honey doesn't spill. In one square inch, bees build 27 worker cells, or 19 drone cells. Somehow the worker bees know that larger or smaller cells are not adequate for raising young bees. This sophisticated design provides strength without using a lot of wax. If we were to stack 3,000 cell walls on top of one another, the stack would be less than 1 inch (2.5 cm) tall. Nevertheless, one pound of beeswax is strong enough to hold 22 pounds (9.9 kg) of honey.

Fanning ● During the hot summer months, bees fan the hive. They do this for two reasons: (1) to evaporate the moisture from the nectar so that it changes into honey, and (2) to cool the hive so that the wax won't melt. The number of fanning bees varies from a few to several hundred, depending on the temperature. If there are just a few, they position themselves outside the hive on the alighting board, face the hive, and beat their wings rapidly. Air currents rush into the hive. If it is very hot, additional bees, with their backs toward the hive, beat their wings on the opposite side of the hive, and the hive quickly cools. Now, how is that for air conditioning!

Making a honeycomb

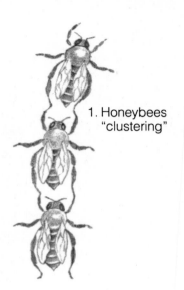

1. Honeybees "clustering"

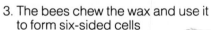

2. Wax oozes out of eight tiny openings on the underside of the abdomen

3. The bees chew the wax and use it to form six-sided cells

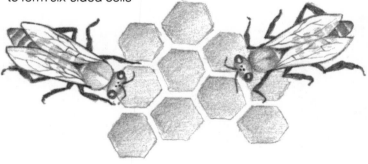

Worker honeybee fanning the hive entrance

Guarding ● One of the last jobs young bees have before they begin to work in the field is that of guarding the hive. Bees entering the hive are scrutinized by the guards from one to three seconds. Guards stand on four feet and hold their front legs up and their antennae forward. If something excites them, they open their mouths, spread their wings, and prepare to attack. If a bee from another hive returns to their hive by mistake and has a load of pollen or nectar, the guards will let her pass. But if such a bee arrives with no load, the guards attack the robber with their stings.

JOBS OUTSIDE THE HIVE

At the age of three weeks, spring and summer bees begin their work in the fields. From sunup to sundown, they fly. If they are lucky, and are not killed in the line of duty, they may live an additional three or four weeks. But gradually the hard work takes it toll. Their wings become frayed and useless. Most die in the field, almost as if they planned it so that their sisters wouldn't have to drag their dead bodies out of the hive.

Bees collect pollen, nectar, water, and propolis (see later). No matter how many loads a bee brings back in the course of the day, her departure from the hive is signaled by the following maneuvers: She cleans her proboscis with her forefeet, rubs her eyes, and cleans her antennae. After she has "washed," she heads for the field again.

Gathering Food ● In Chapter 2, we learned how bees collect pollen in their baskets and store nectar in their honey stomachs. When a bee has a full load of pollen, she returns to the hive and finds a cell. She holds on to one edge of the cell with her forelegs, rests the top of her abdomen on the opposite edge, and pushes the pollen out of her sacs with her middle legs while letting her hind legs dangle into the cell. When a field bee returns to the hive with a load of nectar, she opens her mouth and lets a house bee sip the nectar.

Gathering Water ● To collect water, the bee sips it with her proboscis and carries it back to the hive. She then deposits the droplets over the combs. Extra water is probably stored within a bee's honey stomach.

Gathering Propolis ● Field bees also collect propolis. Propolis, or "bee glue," is a sticky substance secreted by trees and plants that is used by bees to seal rough places and cement movable parts of the hive. To collect propolis, the bee pulls it away, as if it were taffy, from the plant or tree and chews on it, taking care not to become entangled in the goo. She packs her pollen sacs with the mess and returns to the hive. Unable to remove the propolis by herself, she waits for another bee to tear it away from the sacs and immediately spread it on the desired area.

Propolis is most often collected on warm days. This keeps it soft. But occasionally, in the late afternoon, when a bee returns to the hive, the propolis has already dried and hardened. No amount of tugging removes the sticky glue. The bee appears irritated as she walks stiff-legged around the hive. The next day, the bee sits in the sun for several hours, warming and softening the propolis, so that it can be removed and used.

Robbing ● When food is scarce, bees will sometimes rob another hive of honey. Before these robbers land, they fly

Workers blocking the entrance to the hive
with propolis to keep out drafts in winter

back and forth in front of the hive, trying to confuse the guards. Bees are very sensitive to any movement. If the robber bees make it past the guards without getting killed, they gorge themselves on honey. With their sweet booty, they fly back to their own hive.

NAPPING

One activity of bees that does not involve work is napping. If there is a shortage of nectar and pollen, and if the bees are not busy, they will often crawl into a cell for a little catnap. Their heart slows down as they rest. After napping, bees appear to stretch and scratch their heads. Sound familiar?

THE HIVE IN WINTER

During the fall and winter months, life in the hive slows down. The queen lays fewer eggs. Flowers are harder to find, and there is not enough nectar and pollen for the workers to collect. The bees have to live on the supply of honey that they produced during warmer months. To prolong this food, the worker bees drag most of the drones out of the hive to die.

The primary concern of the bees during these months is to keep warm. Thousands of tiny bees join their legs together and rapidly beat their wings. It is warmer in the center of the cluster. Therefore, the bees on the colder, outer edges continually exchange places with those in the middle.

Beekeepers have employed many styles of beehives over the years.

Worker bees born in the winter months live longer. Bees that hatch in the fall have a lifespan of six months.

DESCRIPTION OF THE HIVE

Bees can live in almost anything. Wild bees frequently live in hollow trees, but they will live anywhere as long as they have enough space to make honeycomb cells. Humans have kept bees in many kinds of hives. Skeps, or straw baskets, have been used for centuries and are still used in certain parts of the world. Bees have also been kept in hollow logs with a board hammered to the top and bottom. But skeps and hollow logs make it difficult for a beekeeper to observe the activities of the hive. And, to collect the honey, the beekeeper has to kill the bees.

The modern hive revolutionized beekeeping. It was developed in 1851 by an American, the Reverend L. L. Langstroth. Inside wooden rectangular boxes, Langstroth hung ten movable frames that were separated by a space of approximately ¼ of an inch. In such a hive, combs can be inspected easily and bees do not have to be killed in order to collect the honey.

The Langstroth hive consists of an outer cover, an inner cover, several rectangular wooden boxes, and a bottom board. Resting on the bottom board is the brood chamber box. A queen excluder, which prevents the queen from leaving the brood chamber, may be used to separate the brood chamber from the honey supers. Honey is stored in the honey supers. When needed, beekeepers can add extra brood chambers or honey supers to the hive. Today, millions of beekeepers throughout the world use the Langstroth hive.

COMMUNICATION

Do bees talk to one another? That is, do they communicate in any way? Well, yes, as a matter of fact they do. When a scout bee discovers a source of nectar, she returns to the hive and tells the other bees where the nectar is located, how far away it is, how much is there, and what kind of nectar it is. She even tells the other bees what time of day the nectar is available. That is all pretty amazing when you consider that a bee's brain is no larger than a grain of millet (or less than half the size of a single grain of rice).

How do bees communicate? They dance!

Now, wait a minute. They don't put on little tap shoes and click across the combs. But they do perform a series of dancelike movements with their bodies. The other bees cluster around the dancing bee. They don't really watch the dancing bee. Insect eyes are not as developed as human eyes. The message is understood through touch, sound, odor, and perhaps electrical signals. Scientists can explain the detailed movements, or dances of bees, but they can't yet fully explain how bees communicate through their senses.

This chapter will examine the dances of bees. It will describe how each dance is performed, but it will not explain how the message is understood. There are many puzzles in the universe, and this is one such puzzle for humans. Perhaps someday you will grow up to be an entomologist and delve into the mysteries of insect communication.

BEE DANCES

During the 1920s a German named Karl von Frisch began to investigate how bees communicate. Since that time von Frisch and other scientists have identified the round dance; wag-tail dance; crescent, or sickle, dance; alarm dance; cleaning dance; joy dance; and the massage dance. For his research, von Frisch was awarded the Nobel Prize in 1973.

Round Dance ● When a scout bee discovers nectar less than 100 yards or so (91.4 m) from the hive, she will perform the round dance. As soon as she deposits her load in the hive, she goes to the busiest section of the comb and whirls around in a small circle. Suddenly bees stretch out their antennae and touch the tip of her abdomen. The scout bee dances, and the other bees, in order to keep in touch, whirl around after her. The dance may last for a few seconds or for as long as a minute. The round dance performance does not identify the location of the nectar, for bees rush out of the hive and search in all directions. The message this dance conveys is, "There is food close to home."

Wag-Tail Dance ● The wag-tail dance is performed when the food is more than 100 yards (91.4 m) from the hive. It communicates the distance to and the direction of the food source. The dance begins with the bee making a narrow half-circle, turning sharply, then running in a straight line to the starting point. She continues the dance by making a narrow half-circle in the opposite direction and retracing the straight line path. Each time she gets to the straight run path, she vigorously wiggles her body.

Both the straight run and the waggling tail communicate the distance to the nectar. When the food source is 650 yards (593 m) away, the bee will complete seven runs every fifteen seconds. When the food source is 6,600 yards (6,000 m) away, the bee completes two straight runs every fifteen seconds. In other words, the further the food is from the hive, the fewer runs are made.

While she is waggling her tail, the bee is also making a series of sounds that are inaudible to humans. These sounds may also help to tell the distance to the food.

Distance (yards)	Straight Runs per 15 Seconds
100	9–10
650	7
1,000	4
6,600	2

The direction of the straight run indicates the location of the food source. When the straight run path goes straight up on the brood comb, the food is in the direction of the sun. When the straight run path goes down the brood comb, the food is in the opposite direction from the sun. When the bee angles the straight run to the precise direction, the food is either to the right or left of the sun. Just imagine calculating the sun's position and dancing, all in the darkness of the hive!

Crescent, or Sickle, Dance ● Scout bees do not abruptly stop the round dance at 100 yards (91.4 m) and begin the wag-tail dance. Instead, there is a transition dance called the crescent, or sickle, dance. This dance is performed when the food is more than 10 yards (9.14 m) but less than 100 yards (91.4 m) from the hive. The U-shape pattern formed in the middle of the dance indicates the direction of the food source. The number of waggle movements indicates the distance; the number of waggle movements increases as the distance increases. At approximately 100 yards (91.4 m), the crescent dance evolves into the wag-tail dance.

Whatever the dance may be, an important part of the communication is "listening." The other bees do not rush out in search of the food each time a scout bee performs a dance. They may wait a few hours or even a day before they leave the hive. They participate in the dances of many scout bees. Finally, after "listening" to many bees, they decide which scout bees have found the most nectar, and they leave the hive in search of the source.

The round, wag-tail, and crescent dances are all used to indicate a nectar source. Variations of these dances are performed to announce a source of pollen or propolis or a new nesting site. In addition to these dances, scientists have observed the alarm, cleaning, joy, and massage dances. Although the dance names are descriptive, very little is known as to why these dances are performed.

Alarm Dance ● During the alarm dance, the dancing bee rapidly shakes her abdomen from side to side and runs either in an irregular zigzag motion or a spiral-like pattern. The other bees respond to the dance by immediately stopping all flights. Various disturbances may trigger this dance. A scout bee that gathers nectar contaminated with insecticide is one cause of this dance.

Cleaning Dance ● Whether or not the cleaning dance is the result of a particle of dust or a tiny mite or another cause is unknown. What is known is that the dancer will rapidly stamp her legs and swing her body from side to side. At the same time, she lowers and raises her body, while her middle legs clean the base of her wings. The closest bee touches the dancer with her antennae and cleans the dancer's body with her mouth. The dancer bends toward the cleaner as if to help.

Joy Dance ● The jerking dance and the DVAV (dorso-ventral-abdominal vibration) are two other names for the joy dance. The dancer places her front legs on another bee, then shakes her abdomen five or six times while slightly moving forward and backward. The second bee remains still. The dancer repeats this dance with several bees. Scientists have seen this dance performed in all seasons, at all times of the day or night, on top of queen cells, and during starvation. The ages of the dancers vary widely, but most are older bees.

Massage Dance ● The massage dance begins when a bee holds her head in a particular way. This excites the bees nearby, and they immediately climb over and under her. They pull her leg joints and touch her sides with their antennae, mouth, and front legs. The first bee cleans her extended tongue with her front legs. Sometimes the other bees will clean her tongue for her. After several minutes the dance stops, and the first bee begins to act normally. The massage dance usually occurs during the fall or winter seasons, but it has been observed in the early spring with chilled bees.

6

BEEKEEPING

Beekeeping can be an exciting hobby. It can let you see for yourself many of the things we have talked about in this book. You can observe bees gathering nectar and pollen and returning to the hive. You can observe bees guarding the entrance. You can observe young bees trying out their wings for the first time. On a warm spring day, you might even see drones racing to court the queen.

Just observing nature is rewarding in itself. But there are other reasons for beekeeping. Honeybees are kept for the honey they produce. They are also kept so they can pollinate our crops. In this chapter you will be introduced to the art and science of beekeeping.

GETTING STARTED

There are three ways to obtain bees. One, you can purchase the bees and hive from someone else. Two, you can catch a wild swarm. Three, you can purchase a package of bees.

The first way has its disadvantages. The bees may have

a disease that has contaminated the hive. Or, the hive may be old.

The major drawback to the second way is that it isn't easy for a beginner to catch bees. The third way is not without risks but may be the best way to get started.

If you buy a package of bees, you must choose a particular kind. The three races of honeybees are European, Oriental, and African. American honeybees are descendants of European honeybees, first brought to the New World in 1620. The European race is composed of the Italian, Caucasian, Carniolian, and the dark bees of northern Europe. Many beekeepers prefer Italian honeybees because they are relatively gentle, are resistant to European foul brood disease, and are good collectors of nectar.

Order your bees in the winter and request that they be shipped at the time of the first nectar flow in your geographical area. You should then have eight to twelve weeks to prepare for their arrival. Begin by reading about beekeeping. Check with your school library, public library, bookstore, and your state's agricultural department for books and pamphlets.

EQUIPMENT

The basic equipment for beekeeping includes the hive, clothing, and tools. You will need:

(1) a standard 10-frame hive with frames and comb foundation;

(2) a bee veil that fits snugly around a hat and completely covers your face and neck;

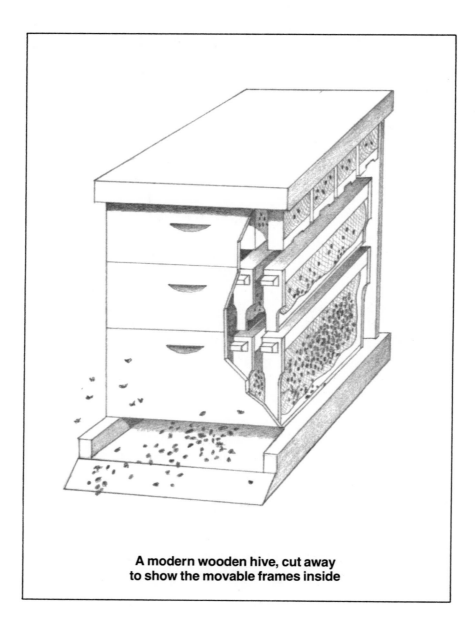

**A modern wooden hive, cut away
to show the movable frames inside**

(3) bee gloves;

(4) light-colored clothing with pant legs tied firmly around your ankles;

(5) a bee smoker so that you can calm the bees before you work with them;

(6) a hive tool so that you can pry the hive and frames apart;

(7) a bee brush for gently removing bees from equipment;

(8) a feeder for offering the bees sugar syrup until they begin gathering nectar.

In addition to this basic equipment, you might want to consider additional purchases. A bee blower blows bees off the equipment. A queen excluder prevents the queen but not the workers from moving up the hive. A frame grip allows you to pick up a frame with one hand rather than two.

Several companies manufacture beekeeping equipment as well as sell bees. Look in the yellow pages of the telephone directory under "Beekeeper Supplies." If there are companies listed you might be able to purchase your equipment locally. If there are no listings, write to some of the companies listed below and request a free catalog.

(1) Maxant Industries, P.O. Box 454, Ayer, Maine 01432

(2) Sears, Roebuck and Co., Sears Tower, Chicago, Illinois 60684 (Ask for a copy of the *Farm and Ranch* catalog.)

(3) Bee-Jay Farm, 1524 Drowning Creek Road, Dacula, Georgia 30211

(4) A. I. Root Co., 623 West Liberty Street, P.O. Box E, Medina, Ohio 44256

(5) Dadant & Sons, Inc., Hamilton, Illinois 62341

Select a good site for your hive. Choose a high location in an open field that is near food sources and fresh water. Trees or shrubs shield the hives from the north wind in winter and provide afternoon shade in the summer. Discourage vandals from molesting the hives by keeping the bees relatively near your home.

EXTRACTING THE HONEY

Finally the day will arrive when it is time to extract the honey. Remove the frame and take it into a honey room (a room that contains the beekeeper's equipment). Carefully slice away the wax covering. Then place the frames into a machine called an extractor. The extractor uses centrifugal force, whirling the frame round and round and throwing the honey out of the cells. The honey drips down to the bottom and is ready to process and store. Ah, the sweet taste of your first crop of honey!

OTHER PRODUCTS
OF THE HIVE

Although honey is the major product of the hive, other bee products include pollen, royal jelly, propolis, bee venom, bees (brood), and beeswax. Propolis, the sticky, gummy material

Beekeepers wear protective clothing and headgear and use a smoker to calm bees.

that fills cracks, is used by veterinarians in the Soviet Union to treat cuts and wounds. Bee venom has been used to treat rheumatoid arthritis. Occasionally, bee brood is used as feed for birds, small mammals, poultry, and fish.

Second to honey, beeswax is the most profitable product of the hive. Cosmetic creams, lotions, lipsticks, and rouge contain beeswax. Candles are made from beeswax. Beeswax is an ingredient in waterproofing materials, floor polishes, and leather. Small portions of beeswax are found in adhesives, crayons, chewing gum, inks, and ski wax.

CROP POLLINATION

One of the greatest services that honeybees perform for humans occurs outside the hive, as the bees travel from flower to flower and gather nectar and pollen. Pollen from the previous flower drops off the bee onto the next flower. This process is called cross-pollination. Thanks to cross-pollination, over $8 billion worth of fruits and vegetables are grown in the United States. Recent studies have shown that as many as ninety crops in the United States are pollinated by honeybees. A few of these crops are apples, pears, cherries, peaches, plums, almonds, blueberries, cranberries, strawberries, avocados, beans, and soybeans. This simple act of the honeybees—gathering nectar and pollen for their own food—gives us not only honey but also a wide variety of foods to eat. This is quite a wonderful feat for such a small creature!

TREATMENT OF STINGS

No book on beekeeping would be complete without a section on the treatment of stings. The first thing to remember is to

Bee in a hollyhock. Bees pollinate many food crops as well as flowering plants.

try to avoid all stings! Bees sting as a defense mechanism when they are alarmed. Your goal is to keep the bees as calm as possible. This is why using a smoker is so important. The smoke is a danger signal that causes the bees to quickly ingest honey in preparation to flee. Bees with full stomachs calm down. Therefore, you can work at the hive soon after you use a smoker. Nevertheless, wear protective clothing in case the smoke doesn't soothe all of the bees.

A bee with stinger exposed

If you still get stung, do not remove the sting by pinching. If you do, the poison will be released in your body. Instead, *carefully* flick the stinger out with the point of a knife blade or your thumbnail.

Most people are not allergic to bee stings. They will itch and possibly swell in the affected area. The best treatment is to keep still and to apply hot towels to the injury. Alternate the hot towels with cold ones.

There are some people, however, who are highly allergic to bee stings. In fact, if they are not desensitized by a doctor, they may die from being stung. If you are ever stung and have difficulty breathing, get medical treatment immediately.

DISEASES AND ENEMIES

It isn't easy to be a bee. Bees can quite easily become sick and die. Various animals and insects like to eat bees and honey. Other animals and insects, because they like to live in beehives, destroy combs and kill the bees. But by far some of the most dangerous creatures known to honeybees are humans. Certain pesticides that are sprayed on plants kill unwanted insects as well as honeybees. Beekeepers spread infection when they do not regularly care for beehives. This chapter will examine the causes, characteristics, and control of specific diseases found in young bees and in adult bees. It will also identify enemies of bees.

BROOD DISEASES

Brood diseases occur in young bees that have not yet emerged from the cells. Adult bees are immune to brood diseases. Some of these brood diseases are American foul brood, European foul brood, sacbrood, and chalkbrood.

The name American foul brood (AFB) does not imply that the disease is found solely in the Americas, nor is European foul brood (EFB) restricted to European bees. Both diseases are found throughout the world. The word "foul," however, does describe the smell generated by both diseases. In the latter stages, AFB has a distinctly foul odor similar to rotting animal flesh. EFB produces a sour yeast- or vinegar-like smell in its earlier stages. Later on, the stench is similar to the odor of dead fish.

Of all the brood diseases, AFB is the most serious and also is the most common. It is caused by a spore-forming germ called *Bacillus larvae*. The germ can resist boiling water and has been found to lie dormant in equipment for fifty years. The disease spreads by (1) bees depositing contaminated honey in a healthy hive; (2) bees storing honey in cells that once contained diseased brood; and (3) beekeepers using contaminated equipment. When nurse bees feed contaminated honey and pollen to young larvae, the disease attacks the brocd.

AFB has certain distinguishing characteristics. Young bees, almost fully formed, will be found dead in the cells lying on their backs with their tongues sticking upward. After a while, the smelly mass becomes ropy and sticky. When a toothpick is inserted into such a cell, the mass will appear stringy. After a few more days, the decayed substance cannot be removed without destroying the shape of the cells.

The most effective means of controlling American foul brood is also the most drastic. All the bees in the infected hive must first be killed. Then the bees and frames are burned together in a pit. The outer hive is scraped and immersed in a boiling lye solution.

EFB is caused by the germ *Streptococcus pluton* and is generally found in weak hives during the spring. EFB spreads in several ways: (1) by nurse bees feeding larvae honey or pollen contaminated with the bacteria; (2) by larvae hatching in cells containing the bacteria; (3) by diseased bees entering the hive; (4) by cleaning bees spreading the bacteria; and (5) by the beekeeper using contaminated equipment. Most of the young bees die by around the fourth day, while their cell is still uncapped. The larvae change from a glistening white to a pale yellow. The remains appear coiled or twisted and are easily removed from the cell. The best means of controlling EFB is to prevent it through good beekeeping habits. Keep the bees protected from winter weather, see that your bees have plenty of pollen and honey to eat, and keep the colonies strong in number. In some cases, requeening and combining two weak hives may be necessary.

Sacbrood is caused by a tiny virus that is slightly infectious. Although the disease occasionally kills worker and drone brood, it rarely destroys an entire colony. The dead larvae are often found in capped cells and turn yellow, then brown. A larva resembles a small sac when removed from the cell. Usually, the colony recovers from the virus without any help from the beekeeper.

Relatively little is known about chalkbrood, which is caused by the fungus *Ascophaera apis*. Sealed larvae or young pupae are covered with filaments that have a fluffy, cottonlike appearance. Bees are usually able to eliminate this disease without beekeeper help.

ADULT BEE DISEASES

To a certain extent, adult bee diseases are not as serious to a bee colony as brood diseases. But they are more difficult to identify since, in the last stages, many of them resemble brood diseases. In the United States, nosema is the most serious. Some of the minor diseases are septicemia, dysentery, and paralysis. In other parts of the world, acarine disease, spread by a microscopic mite, causes severe damage to bees.

Nosema is caused by the protozoan parasite *Nosema apis*, found in contaminated water and honey. The parasite thrives in the bee's stomach and intestine. Because the bees are robbed of the necessary food nutrients, dysentery develops, and the bees eventually die. Right before death, bees make trembling movements and are unable to fly. Their wings become unhooked and their abdomen swells. They also defecate inside the comb. Bees cleaning up the contaminated cells spread the infection throughout the hive.

The best method of controlling nosema is through prevention. Hives should be placed in sunny places and protected from wind so that on cool spring days the bees will leave the hive to defecate. There should be fresh, clean water and plenty of honey available. Soiled combs should be sterilized.

Pesticides also kill a number of bees. Symptoms of pesticide poisoning include an excessive number of dead bees, a lack of worker bees gathering nectar and pollen, and a number of paralyzed, stupefied bees. Care should be given to selecting a pesticide that is not dangerous to bees and in selecting a safe method of applying the pesticide. Sprays and granules are less harmful to bees than is dusting. Use ground equipment to apply the pesticide, and do it at a time when the bees are not working the field, preferably at night.

INSECTS AND
OTHER ENEMIES

Although robber flies, mantids, hornets, wasps, dragonflies, spiders, toads, and birds eat bees, they do not pose a severe

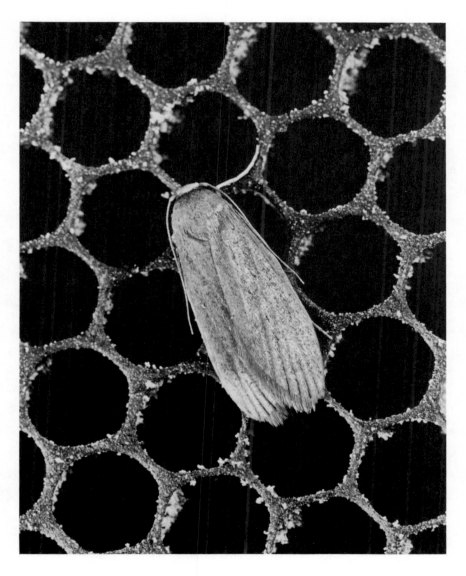

The wax moth, a natural enemy of bees, on a honeycomb

It seems that bears love honey almost as much as humans and are quite willing to risk getting stung while trying to steal it from hives.

threat to the beehive. Only one insect is capable of producing serious damage, and that is the greater wax moth. The female greater wax moth lays its eggs in the cracks of beehives. After the eggs hatch, the larvae tunnel into the wax comb, trailing a webbing of silk strands. As a result, the comb is destroyed, and neither it nor the honey may be sold. Greater wax moths are often found in stored honeycombs. They are controlled by keeping the stored combs in a very cold, well-ventilated room. The best means of controlling them in an active hive is to keep the colony strong and let the bees drag the moths out of the hive.

Bears, skunks, and mice also create havoc for bees and beekeepers. Bears like to eat honey and brood comb and nearly always destroy the hive. If bears live in your area, an electric fence surrounding the hives may be used but is very expensive.

Mice like to spend the winter in beehives. Their nest building wrecks the wax combs. The best way to keep out mice is to make certain that hive entrances are no bigger than the size of a bee.

Skunks eat bees. They enjoy taking an evening stroll to a beehive, scratching on the entrance, and eating the bees that come to the door. Some beekeepers attach a screen above the entrance that discourages the skunk from scratching. If the skunk climbs on top of the screen, the bees will sting the skunk on its belly. So much for a pleasant midnight snack!

8

KILLER BEES

You are sitting in the library at a table reading this book. Suddenly you hear a loud buzzing noise. Your eyes glance up from the words on this page, and you see thousands of bees beating against the library door. Somehow the door opens. The buzzing sound grows louder and louder as the bees rush straight for you. Angry bees cover your body. They are in your ears, your nose, your eyes. The pain of thousands of furious bees stabbing their stings into your body is unbearable. You open your mouth to cry out in pain, and bees rush down your throat, stinging you. You drop your book (carefully) as you claw your eyes with your fingers. You push the table aside and try to run away. The bees are everywhere.

This man wearing a beard of bees doesn't seem to fear being stung. However, it is not *recommended that you try to imitate his stunt.*

There is no escape. You gasp your last breath of air as you sink to the floor.

What you just read was fiction. Many people have made up stories about killer bees. Comedians have done skits about them. Perhaps you've seen a science fiction movie starring them. There have even been news reports about them that weren't entirely accurate.

Are you beginning to wonder what is true and not true about these dreaded creatures? This chapter will identify the known facts on the killer bees: their origin, their characteristics, and how they threaten U.S. agriculture.

The killer bees, or Africanized bees, as scientists prefer to call them, were brought to Brazil from the lowland tropics of Africa during the 1950s. The scientific name for these bees is *Apis mellifera scutellata* (formerly *adansonii*).

Bees derived from European honeybees did not thrive in the tropics of Brazil. Because the climates of Brazil and Africa were similar, a scientist and beekeeper by the name of Dr. Warwick Kerr decided he would be able to import the species *Apis mellifera scutellata* to Brazil.

In 1956, Dr. Kerr arrived in Africa and carefully selected and shipped home 133 gentle but hardworking African queen honeybees. By the time the bees arrived in Brazil, they were all dead. Running short of time, Dr. Kerr quickly sent another shipment of queen bees. This time he did not determine whether or not the chosen bees were aggressive. Forty-seven of them survived the trip.

The bees were extremely vicious, and although Dr. Kerr had planned to give the queens to Brazilian beekeepers, he kept them, intending to improve them genetically by breeding the queens with gentle drones.

He never got the chance.

The African "killer" bee

An unknown beekeeper allowed twenty-six queen bees and their swarms to escape. For several years, the mistake was covered up, and only when the bees began attacking people and animals did Dr. Kerr disclose what had happened.

Several characteristics distinguish Africanized honeybees from the European honeybees. Africanized worker bees (1) take less time to develop from egg to adult, (2) are smaller in size, and (3) have a shorter lifespan than European worker bees. They appear more nervous in the combs and at the hive entrance and move in a pronounced zigzag fashion between flowers.

Africanized bees that forage (hunt) for food are quicker, work longer hours, and can work at night. When food is scarce, they continue to forage after the European bees have stopped. Proportionate to their weight, Africanized bees store two-thirds less honey than European bees do.

It is not these characteristics, however, that threaten the future of beekeeping in North and South America. Beekeepers who work with Africanized bees are confronted with three major problems. These bees (1) sting more often, (2) swarm more often, and (3) abscond more often (see below).

Africanized bees are sensitive to vibrations. Any vibration may trigger a violent reaction. Thousands of bees may respond when the hive is disturbed. They pursue their victims, in order to sting them, far longer than European honeybees. Beekeepers must separate Africanized bees from houses and from other animals by more than 100 yards (91.4 m). And, when working at the hive, beekeepers must wear extra-heavy protective clothing.

Beekeepers could adjust to bees that sting more often. But it is nearly impossible for them to adjust to the Africanized bees' tendencies to swarm and abscond. Swarming means that a group of bees leaves the parent hive to establish a second hive. Absconding means that all of the bees abandon the hive. These characteristics can virtually bring honey production to a halt. After absconding, there are no bees whatsoever. Furthermore, Africanized bees don't fly just a short distance away. One beekeeper tracked a group of them for nearly 200 miles (320 km).

A swarm of honeybees

In addition to excessive swarming and absconding, the Africanized bees also have a high reproductive rate. As a result, they have extended their range approximately 300 miles (480 km) a year. They are now the dominant bees in South America. They achieved their superiority by either killing the local bees or by mating with them. The subsequent generations of bees have displayed Africanized traits. In the countries that have Africanized bees, honey production and beekeeping have decreased dramatically.

The rapid rise of Africanized bees has been carefully monitored by the U.S. Department of Agriculture. Dr. Orley Taylor of the University of Kansas, who directs the department's investigation, and his colleagues predicted that the bees would travel through Central America and Mexico and arrive in the United States in the area of Brownsville, Texas, as early as 1990.

But the Africanized bees beat that prediction by five years. In the summer of 1985, they were discovered in southern California. Scientists theorized that the bees had come to California from South America by ship. The year-old colony was discovered 150 miles (240 km) north of Los Angeles, in the oilfields of Kern County. State and federal officials launched an intense search in an effort to destroy any colonies of the Africanized bees.

It appears that all of the invading Africanized bees have now been killed, but that does not eliminate the potential threat. The bees are still expected in Texas and will spread out from there.

The Africanized bees thrive in a tropical climate. More than likely, they will not be able to survive the cold winters of the northern United States. They are, however, able to survive milder climates. Studies have shown that they can endure freezing temperatures for approximately sixty days. Unfortunately, several states have winters favorable to Africanized bees. These are California, Arizona, Texas, Louisiana, Mississippi, Alabama, North Carolina, South Carolina, Virginia, and Florida.

If and when the Africanized bees arrive in the United States, there are a few safety rules to remember: (1) Do not disturb the bees. (2) Inform the proper authorities of the location of nests or swarms. (3) If the bees become agitated, release penned animals and seek shelter. (4) Escape is possible by quickly running away from an attacking swarm.

Although the Africanized bees may sting in larger numbers than European bees, this behavior is not considered a major hazard to the public. The Department of Agriculture does not want the Africanized bee in the United States for two main reasons. If these bees invade the country, officials fear a decline in honey production and in crop pollination. Not only would beekeepers and farmers suffer a financial loss, but we could also have less honey, fruits, and vegetables to eat.

9

BEE HUNTS

There are deer hunters, bear hunters, dove hunters, safari hunters, whale hunters, and fishers. Most of these hunters need specialized equipment and enough money to get to the appropriate river, countryside, or ocean. But there is another hunter whose bravery deserves mention. This hunter, aside from bravery, requires nothing but a little patience and a free Saturday afternoon. Who is this hunter? Why, a bee hunter, of course!

The purpose of bee hunting is not to kill bees. A dead bee will be of no use to you. Rather, you want the bee to live, for you intend to catch her, feed her, let her go, then follow her back to the hive. If she returns to a hive in the wild and not a hive owned by someone, then your hunt is a success. You have captured what you wanted from the hunt—honey!

Ask your parents first for permission to go on a bee hunt. And take these precautions: wear protective clothing and don't go at all if you are allergic to stings or if there are Africanized bees in your area. Instead, read this chapter and daydream.

Your equipment should include a box, some honey for bait, a pencil, paper, and perhaps a set of binoculars.

Any box will do, but experienced bee hunters prefer one designed in this manner: Cut a hole on top of the box. Over the hole, place a sliding lid so that you can open and shut the hole. Also cut a small flap on top of the box by making three adjacent slits. You may use this flap as a window to watch the bee. Inside the box, set a small container of honey.

Choose a location in the country that is not near any apiaries (bee farms) and one in which you know the area. You do this for two reasons. First, you don't want to follow a bee that belongs to a beekeeper. Second, you don't want to follow a bee and get lost.

Bees can often be found on flowers. When you spot a bee on a flower, slowly move toward it with the lid of your box open. Quickly slap the bee into the box and shut the lid. For a short time, the bee will buzz angrily. But once she discovers the honey, she will calm down and eat. Carry the box to a clearing and set it on something above the ground, such as a stump or a fence post. Then, after you have observed the bee through the window and you are certain that she has had time to fill her honey stomach, slide open the lid to release her.

Watch carefully. After a few minutes the bee will come out of the box, but she will probably return to eat some more. Finally, when her honey stomach is completely filled, she will execute a series of half-circles and figure-eights around the box and the surrounding area, in order to memorize it. Soon she will set off in a particular direction, weaving back and forth. When you can barely see her, she will return halfway. After that, she will make a "beeline" for the hive.

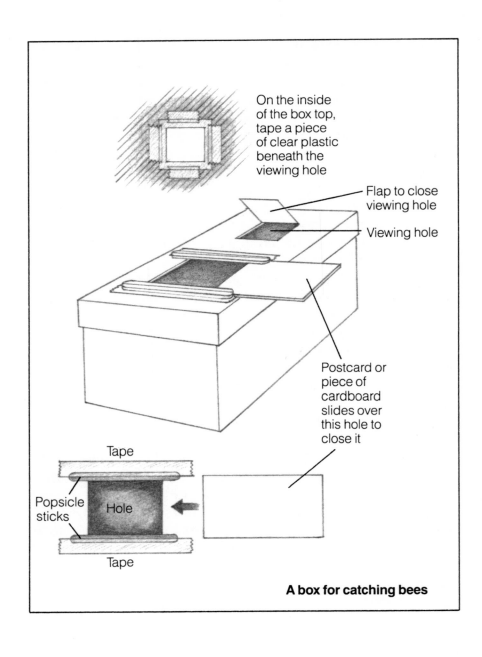

On the inside of the box top, tape a piece of clear plastic beneath the viewing hole

Flap to close viewing hole

Viewing hole

Postcard or piece of cardboard slides over this hole to close it

Tape

Popsicle sticks

Hole

Tape

A box for catching bees

You must wait where you are. The bee will return to the hive, unload the honey, inform the other bees about the food, and return to your box. If the hive is a half-mile (0.8-km) away, the trip will take about eight minutes. While you are waiting, draw a rough map of the area and the direction of the beeline.

By the time you have finished your map, another bee should have arrived at your box. She, too, will eat the honey. It won't take her as long to finish and return to the hive. Watch to see whether she follows the direction of the first bee.

After observing this for several times, you are now ready for your second maneuver. Try to capture two bees in the box, shut the lid, and run with the box as fast as you can at a right angle to the beeline. Again set the box on a stump or a fence post, let the bees eat, and release them when they can eat no more. Observe their direction and draw it on your map. The wild honey will be at the point on your map where the two lines intersect.

Start walking toward that point. Look at every tree until you discover the wild colony. You'll know that you have found the treasure if you see a dozen bees guarding the entrance in a hole of a tree.

Stop! Don't climb that tree and grab the honey. You must follow the civilized bee hunter's rules. Carve your initials into the tree. That will signify to other bee hunters that the honey is yours. You must then wait to see if the bees survive the winter months. If they don't, they probably didn't make enough honey for you anyway. If they do survive the winter, ask the owners of the tree if you can cut it down. Tell them you will give them part of the honey and that you will cut the tree into firewood for them.

When you cut down the tree, split it open, rescue the queen, and put her in a new hive. The other bees will follow.

Now, you've followed the bee and found the honey. You've chopped down the tree. You've rescued the bees. There is only one more thing to do. That's right. Eat the honey!

10

COOKING
WITH HONEY

If you are thinking that a bee hunt takes too much time and trouble, there is a simpler way to get honey. Buy it at the store! In no time at all you will be back in your kitchen and ready to make a tasty treat.

People have been cooking with honey for a long time. Honey is healthy, low in bacteria, has traces of vitamins and minerals, and is considered a source of energy. But these are not the reasons that most people eat honey. They eat it because it tastes good.

Honey can be substituted for sugar. Because it is sweeter than sugar, not as much honey is required in recipes. Honey also retains water. As a result, breads, cakes, and cookies made with honey will remain moist longer than those cooked with sugar.

When you cook, it's a good idea to use light-colored honey, since dark honey has a stronger flavor. Another hint is to coat the measuring utensil with oil or butter so that the honey will pour out easily. Try substituting honey for sugar in some of your favorite recipes.

SUBSTITUTING HONEY FOR SUGAR

Bakery Item	Substitution	Comments
Yeast Breads	Measure for measure	
Muffins	Measure for measure	
Cookies (crisp type)	A third of the sugar may be replaced with honey	Reduce oven by 25° F
Brownies	Half of the sugar may be replaced with honey	Reduce oven by 25° F
Cakes	A third of the sugar may be replaced with honey	Reduce oven by 25° F; reduce liquid by ¼ cup for each cup of honey. If recipe does not contain baking soda, add ¼ teaspoon per cup of honey.

Here are a few recipes that include honey as an ingredient. For more recipes using honey, check with health food stores or look for honey cookbooks in bookstores. Or, write to your state's department of agriculture and request free brochures on cooking with honey.

Peanut Butter Banana Honey Sandwich

Spread peanut butter on one slice of bread. Smooth honey over peanut butter. Place sliced bananas on honey. Position another slice of bread on top. Enjoy!

Honey Grapefruit

Cut grapefruit in half and remove center. Pour honey in hole and dribble over grapefruit. Allow to stand a short time before serving.

Strawberry Special

2 tablespoons honey
1 cup sliced strawberries
1 cup yogurt
1 cup milk

In blender, combine ingredients and whip until smooth.

Honey Energy Freeze

1 6-ounce can frozen orange juice concentrate
1¾ cups milk
½ cup mild-flavored honey
1 teaspoon vanilla
7 ice cubes

Place all ingredients except ice in blender. Blend. Increase speed and add ice cubes through feeder cap. Process until ice is liquified and mixture is smooth and thick.

Honey-Brunch Cocoa

1 quart milk
2 sticks cinnamon
¼ cup cocoa
⅛ teaspoon salt
3 tablespoons honey

Scald milk with cinnamon sticks. Mix cocoa and salt; blend in ½ cup hot milk until smooth. Add to scalded milk and stir in honey. Remove the cinnamon sticks. Mix with a rotary beater.

Honey-Baked Chicken

12 pieces of chicken, thighs, legs, and breasts
oil
½ cup light honey
¼ cup soy sauce

Heat some oil in large skillet and brown chicken. Place chicken in greased baking dish. Mix honey and soy sauce and brush chicken pieces. Bake at 200° F for 2 hours. Occasionally brush chicken with mixture.

Glazed Carrots

In saucepan, melt ¼ cup butter or margarine. Add ¼ cup honey and blend. Add 8 cooked carrots (whole or halved lengthwise). Cook over medium heat, turning carrots until well glazed and tender, about 12 minutes.

Mary V's Honey Banana Mold

1 3-ounce package orange gelatin
2 medium bananas
½ cup honey
3 tablespoons lemon juice
⅔ cup evaporated milk

Dissolve gelatin in 1 cup boiling water; cool. Mash bananas in large bowl using electric mixer at medium speed. Blend in honey, lemon juice, and gelatin. Chill until thickened. Chill milk until icy crystals form; beat gradually, at low speed, into gelatin mixture. Turn to high speed; beat until mixture doubles in volume and becomes thick. Turn into lightly oiled 5-cup mold. Chill until set. Unmold.

Aurelia's Honey Nutritional Snack

24 ounces peanut butter
16 ounces powdered milk
1½ cups honey
½ cup sesame seeds
1 cup raisins
1 cup chopped pecans
½ cup wheat germ

Mix ingredients together. Roll in wax paper. Chill. Slice.

Honey Brownies

⅓ cup margarine
⅓ cup sugar

½ cup honey
2 teaspoons vanilla
2 eggs
½ cup flour
⅓ cup cocoa
1 cup pecans

Cream margarine and sugar together. Add honey, vanilla, and eggs. Mix flour and cocoa together well and add to creamed mixture. Add pecans. Bake in a greased 8-inch square pan at 350° F for 30 to 35 minutes.

Egyptian Bread

10 slices white bread, crusts removed
1 pound honey

Soak bread in honey for at least 30 minutes. Place slices in buttered baking dish; layer each evenly over top of one another. Bake at 300° F for 25 minutes. Chill and serve with cream over top.

Honey-Nut Bread

1 cup honey
1 cup milk
¼ cup butter
2 beaten eggs
2½ cups whole wheat flour
1 teaspoon salt
1 tablespoon baking powder
½ cup chopped walnuts

Warm honey and combine with milk. When blended, beat in remainder of ingredients, except for nuts. Fold these in when mixture is blended. Spoon into large greased loaf pan and bake for one hour at 325° F. This is an old recipe. It freezes well.

Honey Butter

Whip together 1 part mild-flavored honey and 2 parts of soft butter. Store in refrigerator.

Honey Cosmetics

(Don't eat this one. It's for your face.)

Mix 1 tablespoon honey with one tablespoon flour. Add a few drops of rose water to make the honey paste smooth and liquid. Clean face, then spread mixture over face. Leave on for 30 minutes. Remove with cold water and cloth.

GLOSSARY

Abdomen—Third, or last, section of bees. Includes the heart, honey stomach, stomach, intestine, reproductive organs, and the stinger.

Abscond—When all of the bees in a hive leave to establish a new colony.

Antenna (plural *Antennae*)—Pair of slender feelers located on the head and containing certain sense organs.

Apiary—A place where beehives are kept.

Apis mellifera—Scientific name for the honeybee, *Apis*, meaning "bee," and *mellifera*, meaning "honey bearing."

Apis mellifera scutellata—Scientific name for the "killer bees," originally from Africa.

Bee bread—Pollen mixed with a small amount of honey that is stored in the comb.

Bee dance—Movement by worker bees on the combs that communicates information.

Bee glue—See Propolis.

Beeline—Shortest distance between two points that the bee flies.

Bee space—Passage of ¼ to ⅜ of an inch between combs in the beehive.

Beeswax—Wax that is secreted from eight holes on the underside of a worker bee's abdomen and that is used to build honeycomb.

Brood—Young, developing bees; includes the stages of egg, larva, and pupa.

Cluster—Bees hanging together by means of hooks on their feet; in winter, bees cluster to stay warm.

Comb foundation—Sheets of beeswax onto which bees build honeycomb cells.

Drone—Male bee.

Extractor—Machine that removes honey from comb by use of centrifugal force.

Feces—Excreta, or droppings, of bees.

Field bees—Worker bees that collect nectar, pollen, propolis, and water.

Foul brood—Contagious disease that affects young bees.

Hive—Home for bees.

Hive tool—Metal tool used to open hives and pry frames apart.

Honey—Sweet food produced by bees; made from the nectar of flowers.

Honeycomb—Mass of hexagonal cells built back to back, the majority of which are worker brood size.

Honey stomach—Sac in the bee's stomach that stores nectar during flight.

Hymenoptera—Order to which all bees belong, as well as ants and wasps, Hymenoptera meaning "membrane wings."

Killer bees—See *Apis Mellifera Scutellata*.

Larva (plural *Larvae*)—Second stage of developing bee brood; worm is unsealed in the cell.

Nectar—Sweet liquid found inside flowers and on plant leaves.

Nosema—Disease of adult bees; parasite infects mid-gut.

Nurse bees—Young worker bees from three to ten days old that feed young larva and work inside the hive.

Pollen—Dustlike grains on anthers of flowers that are needed by other flowers for seed production; also food for young bees.

Pollen basket—Area on hind legs of bees that carries pollen from flower to hive.

Pollination—Transfer of pollen from male to female element of flower.

Proboscis—Tongue, or combined mouth parts of bees.

Propolis—Sticky substance of plants and trees that bees use to close cracks and openings.

Pupa—Third, or last, stage of developing brood in which the young bee is sealed in its cell.

Queen—Sexually developed female bee, the mother bee.

Royal jelly—Food that is secreted by glands in worker bees' heads and fed to young brood.

Super—Boxes in a modern hive. Bottom supers are called brood chambers. Top boxes are called honey supers.

Swarm—When some of the workers, drones, and a queen leave to establish a new colony.

Thorax—Middle section of bees between head and abdomen to which the legs and wings are attached.

Wax glands—Eight glands on worker's abdomen that secrete wax.

Worker bee—Sexually underdeveloped female bee so named because she does almost all of the work in the hive.

FOR FURTHER READING

Blau, Melinda. *Killer Bees.* New York: Raintree, 1977.

Dadant and Sons. *The Hive and the Honey Bee.* Hamilton, Illinois: Dadant and Sons, 1982. (Standard reference book for beekeepers.)

Lecht, Jane. *Honeybees.* Washington, D.C.: National Geographic Society, 1973.

Penner, Lucille Recht. *The Honey Book.* New York: Hastings House, 1980.

Root, A.I. *The ABC and XYZ of Bee Culture.* Medina, Ohio: A. I. Root Co., 1962. (Standard reference book for beekeepers.)

Shebar, Sharon. *The Mysterious World of Honeybees.* New York: Messner, 1979.

INDEX

*Illustrations are indicated
by italicized page numbers*

Abdomen, 17–19
Africanized bees, 72–77
    arrival in South America, 72–73
    arrival in United States, 76, 77
    characteristics of, 73, 75, 76
    and crop production, 76
    reproduction of, 76
    sting of, 75, 77
American foul brood (AFB), 63–64
Antennae, 15–17, 50, 53

Baby bees. *See* Brood
Bears, *68*, 69
Bee bread, 23, 37
Bee brood, 58, 60
Bee glue. *See* Propolis
Bee hives, 46–48.
    See also Beekeeping; Cells; Ho-
    neycombs
Beekeeping, *59*
    Africanized bees, 75
    equipment, 55, 57–58

honey gathering, 58
    obtaining bees, 54–55
Beeswax, 20, 39–40, 58, 60
Blood, 22
Bodies. *See* Abdomen; Blood; Exo-
    skeleton; Eyes; Head; Honey Stom-
    ach; Nervous system; Thorax
Brain, 22, 49
Brood, 23–27, 32, 37
Brood food. *See* Royal jelly

Cells:
    brood cells, 35
    honey storage, 20, 37, *39*, 40
    living quarters, 24
    See also Honeycombs
Chalkbrood, 63, 65
Circulatory system, 22
Cleaning bees, 39
Clustering, 20
Combs. *See* Honeycombs
Communication, 15, 49. *See also*
    Dance
Court. *See* Queen's court
Crop pollination. *See* Cross pollination

Cross pollination, 60, 77

Dance
    alarm dance, 52–53
    cleaning dance, 53
    crescent dance, 52
    joy dance, 53
    massage dance, 53
    round dance, 50, 52
    sickle dance, 52
    wag-tail dance, 50–52
Diet, 15, 23, 35, 37
Diseases:
    adult diseases, 65–66
    brood diseases, 63–65
Dorso-ventral-abdominal vibration
    (DVAV). See Dance, Joy dance
Drones, 23, 24, 32–33. See also
    Brood

Eggs, 17, 19, 23, 25, 30, 37
Enemies, 63, 66–68
European foul brood (EFB), 55, 64–65
Exoskeleton, 13–15
Extractor, 58
Eyes, 12–13, 29, 32, 49

Fanning bees, 40, 42
Flight speed, 16
Frisch, Karl, von, 50

Greater wax moth, 67, 69
Growth, stages of, 23–27
Guard bees, 43, 46

Head, 15
Honey, 12, 37, 58
    and history, 9–10
    as a sugar substitute, 83–84
    recipes, 85–89
Honey stomach, 20, 37, 44

Honeycombs, 39–40, 48
House bees, 37
Hunting bees, 79–81
Hymenoptera, 16

Jerking dance. See Dance, Joy
    dance
Jobs
    brood feeding, 35
    cell polishing, 35
    comb building, 39
    comb cleaning, 39
    of drones, 30–32
    fanning, 49
    food storage, 37
    gathering food, 43–44
    gathering propolis, 44
    gathering water, 44
    guarding, 43
    of queen bees, 19, 20, 23
    of worker bees in hives, 35–43
    of worker bees outside hives, 43–
    46

Kerr, Warwick, 72–73
Killer bees. See Africanized bees

Langstroth, L.L., 48
Larvae, 23–24, 25
Legs, 16–17
Lifespan, 48
    drone, 32
    queen, 29
    workers, 43

Mating, 29–30
Mice, 69

Napping, 46
Nectar, collection of, 20, 49, 60. See
    also Dance

Nectar, storage of, 20, 37, 44
Nervous system, 22
Nosema, 66
Nurse bees, 37, 64

Parenting, 30, 32
Pesticides, 53, 63, 66
Pollen, 15, 17, 37, 43–44. *See also*
   Cross pollination
Pollen baskets, 17, *18*
Proboscis, 15, 19, 37, 44
Products, 58–60
Propolis, 44, *45*, 58, 60
Pupae, 24, *36*

Queen bee, *24, 26,* 27–32
   job of, 19, 20, 23
Queen's court, 29, 30

Races of honeybees, 55
Recipes, 85–89
Reproduction, 17, 19, 29, 30
   of Africanized bees, 76.
   See also Mating
Rituals, 43, 44, 46, 79. *See also*
   Dance; Jobs; Mating
Robber bees, 44, 46
Royal jelly, 15, 23, 35, 39, 58

Sacbrood, 63, 65
Scientific name, 9
Scout bees, 49, 50, 52
Senses, 15, 49. *See also* Eyes
Sex determination, 30
Skeleton. *See* Exoskeleton
Skeps, 48
Skunks, 69
Smoke, 61
Stinger, *62*
Stings, 20–22, 29
   of Africanized bees, 75, 77
   treatment of, 60–62
Stomach. *See* Honey stomach
Straight run, 51
Sugar substitution, 83–84
Supply companies, 57–58

Thorax, 16–17

Venom, 60

Water, 44
Wax glands, 20
Wings, 16
Winter, 46
Worker bees, 12–13, 23, *24, 31, 38,*
   42, 45. See also Brood